Celebrate
Ramadan

Laura S. Jeffrey

Pakistani girls share an 'Id greeting outside
the Badshahi Mosque in Pakistan.

Enslow Publishers, Inc.
40 Industrial Road
Box 398
Berkeley Heights, NJ 07922
USA

http://www.enslow.com

The editor would like to thank the
Council on Islamic Education for its academic input.

Copyright © 2008 by Enslow Publishers, Inc.

Library of Congress Cataloging-in-Publication Data

Jeffrey, Laura S.
   Celebrate Ramadan / Laura S. Jeffrey.
      p. cm. — (Celebrate holidays)
   Includes bibliographical references and index.
   ISBN-13: 978-0-7660-2774-9
   ISBN-10: 0-7660-2774-0
   1. Ramadan—Juvenile literature. 2. 'Id al-Fitr—Juvenile literature.
     3. Fasts and feasts—Islam—Juvenile literature. I. Title.
   BP186.4.J44 2007
   297.3'62—dc22

                        2006028107

Printed in the United States of America

10 9 8 7 6 5 4 3 2 1

To Our Readers:
We have done our best to make sure all Internet Addresses in this book
were active and appropriate when we went to press. However, the author
and the publisher have no control over and assume no liability for the
material available on those Internet sites or on other Web sites they may
link to. Any comments or suggestions can be sent by e-mail to
comments@enslow.com or to the address on the back cover.

Every effort has been made to locate all copyright holders of material used
in this book. If any errors or omissions have occurred, corrections will be
made in future editions of this book.

CONTENTS

Praying, Fasting, Celebrating

It is very early in the morning; the sun has not even risen yet. But young Bushra Hayat is already awake. Bushra was born in Nairobi, Kenya. Now, she and her family live in London, England. Bushra has two older brothers, Rafiq and Laiq, and two younger brothers, Zaheer and Naseer.

Bushra joins her mother and father at the breakfast table. In the dark hours of the morning, Bushra and her family eat a very small meal. Then

Muslim women break their fast after the sun sets on the first day of Ramadan at the Islamic Cultural Center in New York.

they pray. As soon as the sun comes up, the family stops eating. They go about their daily business, but they also fast. To fast means to not eat or drink.

Bushra is just a child. She does not fast the entire day. Her mother tells her she must break

A boy in Karachi, Pakistan, prepares bowls of fruit and other foods for the end of the first day of Ramadan.

the fast and eat lunch. But Bushra's mother and father do not eat again until the sun sets for the day. Even then, it is another small meal. The family also prays some more.

Bushra's family repeats this routine every day for one month. During this time, Bushra is on her best behavior. She tries not to lie, fight, or cause trouble. Just as it might be hard for the adults to fast, it is hard for Bushra to be on her best behavior.[1] However, she knows that during this month, she and her family are becoming closer to Allah, or God. Bushra is also excited.[2] She knows that at the end of the month, she and her family will celebrate a very special holiday.

Bushra helps her mother prepare for this holiday several days before it actually occurs. They cook special foods that they will eat on this day. They buy new clothes to wear to their house of worship. They purchase or make gifts to exchange with family members. They clean the house in anticipation of receiving visitors.

Bushra and her family are Muslims. This means they are followers of the religion known as Islam. The month they spend praying and fasting is called Ramadan. Ramadan is an annual observance. It celebrates a time about fourteen centuries ago when, according to Muslim

Muslim families, such as this one in Los Angeles, California, eat special foods at the end of the day during Ramadan.

belief, God communicated with the prophet Muhammad through the angel Gabriel. These communications led to the establishment of Islam. The holiday that follows Ramadan is called the Festival of Fast Breaking, or 'Id al Fitr.

Bushra is now an adult. She is married to Shahid Malik, who is originally from Lahore,

Pakistan. She immigrated to the United States in 1985. Today, Bushra and her family live in Virginia, near Washington, D.C. Shahid is also a Muslim. Bushra and Shahid have passed their religious traditions down to their own family.

In 2005, Ramadan took place in October. While many other American families watched football games on TV or participated in Halloween

In Brooklyn, New York, Muslims celebrate at Prospect Park.

festivities, the Malik family observed Ramadan. The youngest Malik, Sosan, was ten years old. She did not fast, but her siblings did. Brothers Danisch, who was twenty-one years old, and Faiq, who was sixteen, both fasted. So did sister Labeeda, who was seventeen years old.

Muslims come from many different ethnic backgrounds and cultures. What each family decides to eat for Ramadan and 'Id al Fitr is unique. This Ramadan feast from Indonesia features red snapper, salad, chicken, beef, lamb, and rice.

Danisch Malik first started fasting during Ramadan when he was nine years old. Now, he fasts every day of Ramadan. During the 2005 Ramadan, Faiq Malik fasted for twenty-six days. "Labeeda does not have as much stamina as her brother," Bushra said, "but she fasted for fifteen days."[3]

Like she did as a child, Bushra and her family spent part of Ramadan preparing for 'Id al Fitr.

Ramadan and 'Id al Fitr feasts feature traditional Middle Eastern sweets like these.

They celebrated 'Id the day after Ramadan ended. The family donned new clothes and attended a special prayer service at their mosque. Then, they visited with members of their extended family. They ate, relaxed, and exchanged gifts, and the children played.

Ramadan and 'Id al Fitr might not be as well known in the United States as other holidays. After all, stores do not advertise sales for them, as they do for Christmas, Thanksgiving, and other special occasions. However, the number of Muslims in the United States is growing. Around the world, the number of Muslims is very substantial. It is estimated that over one billion people in the world are followers of Islam. The religion embraces all ethnicities: white, black, Asian, Indian, Hispanic, and others.

It is important, then, to learn about Ramadan and 'Id al Fitr, two of the most important events in the Islam religion. The foundation for them is spelled out in Islam's most holy book, the Qur'an. They were detailed about two thousand years ago, to an Arabian man known as Muhammad.

Muhammad's revelations from Allah are recorded in the Muslim holy book called the Qur'an.

Muhammad: God's Final Prophet

The religion of Islam dates back more than fourteen hundred years. Its history begins with a man named Muhammad. Muhammad was born in 570 C.E. in Mecca, a city in modern-day Saudi Arabia near the Red Sea. Muhammad's family belonged to a well-respected tribe. Muhammad was not spoiled, however. His father died before he was born. He was put in the care of his grandfather and then his uncle. He was sincere, honest, and kindhearted.[1] Many of Muhammad's wealthy neighbors were not the same way. They were cruel to people who were less fortunate. They also worshiped many different gods, held superstitious beliefs, and lacked spiritual discipline.[2]

Muhammad became more and more committed to spiritual meditation. Every year, Muhammad retreated to the mountains by himself. During one of these solitary periods, when Muhammad was about forty years old, he received a revelation. A revelation is a communication from a divine being. Muhammad's revelation came from Allah, or God. According to Muslim belief, God sent the angel Gabriel to deliver the revelation to Muhammad. The revelation was that Muhammad was to be a prophet of God.

Gabriel continued to visit Muhammad and share God's revelations, called the Qur'an. The passages of the Qur'an stressed God's power and mercy, instructed people to live more honorable lives, and described the nature of life after death (called the afterlife). Muhammad began telling people about these revelations. Soon, a small following of people accepted the idea that there was only one God.

The revelations of the Qur'an were memorized by Muhammad's followers. They wrote the revelations on parchment, leather, clay, and other

Afterlife

Muslims believe in life after death known as *al-akhirah*.[3] A person's deeds during his or her life determine whether he or she will enter *Janna* (Paradise) or *Jahannam* (Hell). The Qur'an tells of the Last Day, when the world will be destroyed and God raises the dead in order to be judged by Him.[4] Those who were loyal to their faith and performed good deeds will be welcomed into Janna, a place with beautiful gardens, abundant food, splendid thrones, and rivers of pure, clean water, milk, wine, and honey.[5] Those who were bad when they were alive are destined for the fiery torment of Jahannam.[6]

materials. The Qur'an is one leg of two that form the basis of Islam. The other leg is the Hadith, the wording of the Prophet rather than God. *Islam* means "submission to God," or the complete acceptance of the teaching and guidance of God as revealed to the prophet Muhammad.[7] Those who follow Islam are called Muslims, or "those who submit to God."[8] Muslims believe that by accepting and following God's teachings, human beings can achieve peace in their personal lives and in their relationships with others.

Muhammad told people that there was only one God. He also explained that all believers are equals and of a community.[9] Muhammad and his followers were persecuted for their beliefs. This means they were harassed and threatened. Muhammad was forced to leave Mecca. He moved to a city named Medina. There, people were more open to his teachings. He devoted the rest of his life to preaching the word of God and helping the poor.

Muslims do believe that earlier figures such as Noah, Abraham, Moses, David, and Jesus were important prophets of God. But in the Islam religion, Muhammad is considered the final prophet of God.

Muhammad died at the age of sixty-three. According to Islam, he received revelations from God for twenty-three years. All of these revelations form the content of the Qur'an. The revelations are usually arranged from the longest chapter to the shortest.

The Qur'an is considered sacred scripture by Muslims, who believe it to be the literal words of God.[10] Many Muslims memorize the entire Qur'an—which is over six thousand verses—word for word. This ensures the preservation and transmission of the Qur'an from generation to generation. The word "Qur'an" means recitation.

In Pakistan, girls recite verses from the Qur'an
at their religious school.

Muslims believe that reciting the Qur'an is an act of worship, and they try to do so in a melodious voice.

The Qur'an provides a framework for Muslims' core beliefs and religious practices. It contains guidance for forms of worship, the value of community life and family, and the obligations that human beings have to God and one another. For example, the Qur'an instructs Muslims to offer worship to God several times a day, and to fast during certain times of the year. Muslims are to be humble, generous, and just. The Qur'an also stresses that men and women should dress modestly, and they are to remain chaste until marriage. "Chaste" means to remain pure in thoughts and actions.

However, faith and prayer alone are not enough to get into heaven. Muslims believe God is pleased by good deeds. So Muslims must give to those who are less fortunate. They also should help to improve the lives of fellow Muslims as well as members of the community at large. The Qur'an says that God will bring about an end to the present world. Then, there will be a Day of Judgment. Muslims believe God will judge each person who has ever lived according to their own beliefs and circumstances, and will reward or punish them accordingly. The Qur'an states that anyone who believed in God and worked righteously on Earth will be rewarded. Muslims hope to be among that group of people.

The Qur'an is composed of 114 chapters. Each chapter, called a *sura*, has a number and a title.

The Prophet Muhammad lived in what is now Saudi Arabia. It is a country in the part of the world called the Middle East. This is what the area looks like today.

The title usually refers to a word or phrase that occurs early in the chapter.[11] Each sura begins with the words: "In the name of God, the Merciful, the Compassionate." This phrase is also spoken by Muslims at the beginning of every act of worship as well as any important moment in life.[12] These include the night before traveling on a journey, starting a business meeting, or even as a way of "saying grace" before a meal.

In Cairo, Egypt, employees of the Alfa Ceramics Company pray during their work day.

According to the Qur'an, there are five pillars, or core practices, of the religion. The first pillar of Islam, called Shahadah, is a testimony of faith. Followers express their belief that there is no other god except for God, and that Muhammad was God's messenger. This declaration indicates a Muslim's acceptance of *tawhid* (oneness of God), and the desire to follow Muhammad's teachings and example as a way to live a life pleasing to God.

The second pillar is Salah, or prayer. Muslims pray five times a day to God. This is a way for Muslims to acknowledge their creator, express their devotion to him, and seek guidance from him in their personal affairs. Muslims also use these moments to pray for the betterment of the world and humanity at large. Muslims believe prayer helps guard against sin and wrongdoing.

Charitable giving, or Zakah, is the third pillar of Islam. Muslims who have a certain standard of living and possess a surplus of wealth are required each year to give money, goods, or property to the less fortunate. Or, they may make donations to benefit the entire Muslim community.

Fasting during the Islamic month of Ramadan, called Sawm, is the fourth pillar of Islam. It is the ninth month of the Islamic lunar calendar, and it is honored as the month in which Gabriel first

Abraham and Ka'bah

Abraham was the founder of Judaism and the ancestor of the Arabs and Jews. Scholars believe he lived between 1800 and 1500 B.C. He was born Abram in the city of Ur in Mesopotamia, which is now known as Iraq. Unlike all the other people in Ur who believed in many gods, Abram believed there was only one true God, and so God commanded that he and his family settle in the land of Canaan (present-day Palestine). God made an agreement with Abram promising that Canaan would belong to Abram and all of his descendants if they remained faithful to Him. God changed Abram's name to Abraham, meaning "father of many nations," as a symbol of His promise. As a test of Abraham's faith, God commanded that he sacrifice his son Isaac. Abraham would have gone through with it if God had not stopped him at the last minute.[14]

Ka'bah is the most sacred shrine of Islam located near the center of the Great Mosque in Mecca, the Muslims' holiest city. According to Islamic belief, Abraham and his son Ishmael built the Ka'bah and were given the Black Stone by the angel Gabriel. The Black Stone now rests in the eastern corner of the shrine inside a silver ring. Muslims all over the world face in the direction of the Ka'bah when they pray. The Ka'bah is the final destination of the Muslims' annual pilgrimage called hajj. They walk around it seven times while praying and reciting verses from the Qur'an, and touch or kiss the Black Stone at the end of the ceremony.[15]

visited Muhammad in 610 C.E. and revealed the
Qur'an. Fasting in Ramadan helps Muslims
demonstrate their commitment to God; empathize
with those who are poor; and learn self-control,
humility, knowledge, and personal faith.[13]

The fifth pillar of Islam is called Hajj, or
pilgrimage to Mecca. A pilgrimage is a journey to a
holy place. Mecca is the holiest city of Islam
because it is the location of the Ka'bah, a house of
worship built by Abraham in ancient times to
worship God.

When Muhammad returned to Mecca in 632 C.E.
after defeating the Meccan tribes who opposed
him, he cleared the pagan idols that the Arabs had
accumulated there in the centuries after Abraham
died. The hajj rituals instituted by Muhammad
enable Muslims to commemorate the trials of
Abraham and his family and their commitment to
monotheism, or the belief that there is only one God.

According to Islamic teaching, Muslims who
are healthy and financially able should make at
least one pilgrimage in their lifetime. The purpose
is to renew faith by rededicating oneself to God,
and to meet fellow Muslims from other countries
and backgrounds. The hajj helps Muslims feel
connected to each other as an *ummah*, or
worldwide community of believers.

-theisms

While most people are familiar with monotheistic faiths such as Islam, Judaism, and Christianity, all of which believe in one God, there are other kinds of belief systems all around the world. Polytheism is the belief in many gods. In Hinduism, for example, there are three main gods: Brahma, the creator of the universe; Vishnu, its preserver; and Shiva, its destroyer.[18] There are about 33 million other gods and goddesses as well. However, most Hindus also believe that all the gods, or deities, are part of a single universal spirit called Brahman. Many tribal religions accept the idea that there is a supreme God above the gods, so it is a blurred line separating monotheistic and polytheistic religions.[19]

Pantheism is the belief that God exists in all things in nature. Native American, African, and ancient Middle Eastern religions associated gods with things like the sky, the sea, fertility, and hunting prowess. The Japanese Shinto tradition identifies gods with natural objects such as trees and rocks.[20]

The hajj takes place in the twelfth month of the Islamic calendar, called Dhu al-Hijja. The hajj lasts for about ten days, and draws several million Muslims every year. Called Pilgrims, they wear white, seamless clothing.[16] This attire symbolizes purity, peace, and human equality before the eyes of God.

A key event is a mass prayer ceremony on the plains of Arafat outside Mecca. In 632 C.E., Muhammad gave his final sermon on a nearby hill, where he stressed the equality of all humankind, the importance of fulfilling promises, and the need to respect one another's rights.

Anyone who wants to follow Islam may become a Muslim. To convert, he or she says the following words: "La ilaha illa Allah, Muhammadur rasoolu Allah." This means, "There is no god but God, and Muhammad is the Messenger [Prophet] of God."[17]

Muslims have a variety of Arabic spoken traditions. After saying the name of God, or Muhammad, Muslims say, "Subhanahu wa ta'ala." This means, "Praise to the Lord." After saying the name of Muhammad, Muslims say, "Swall-allahu alayhi wa sallam." This means, "Peace be upon him."[21]

Although Islam is a religion of peace, mercy, and forgiveness,[22] many people associate Islam with terrorism. This is primarily because of the interplay between religion and politics, and the way in which political figures such as Osama bin Laden use the language of Islam to advance and justify political causes.

Bin Laden, who was born in Saudi Arabia, is the leader of al-Qaeda, which was formed in the early 1990s by veterans of the Afghan resistance to an invasion by the Soviet Union. Bin Laden was angered by Saudi Arabia's reliance on the United States for protection during the 1990–1991 Gulf War. The United States led this war after Iraq invaded Kuwait. Saddam Hussein, Iraq's leader, claimed Kuwait was historically part of Iraq, and he wanted control of Kuwait's oil supplies. King Fahd of Saudi Arabia was fearful that Iraq would invade his country, too. The king asked the United States for help.

Bin Laden was angry that King Fahd allowed the United States to establish military bases in Saudi Arabia, which were used to launch attacks against Iraqi forces in Kuwait. Bin Laden called the bases an "occupation" of the Arab Holy Land. Fueled by perceptions of U.S. exploitation and injustice in Middle East affairs, al-Qaeda began recruiting fighters and planning deadly attacks against Western interests all over the world. In 1996, bin Laden issued a fatwah, or religious decree, justifying the killing of American "crusaders."[23] In the years that followed, many attacks of terrorism were carried out by bin Laden's followers, or by others who saw the world in the same stark way. These extremists said such attacks made God happy because they were just,

The Taliban

Formed in the early 1990s, the Taliban is a group of conservative Muslims that originated in Islamic schools. The name *Taliban* means "seekers after knowledge."[24] The group formed in an effort to put down the disorder that came from years of war in Afghanistan. They stringently obeyed and imposed Islamic laws, such as making women cover themselves from head to toe. Lawbreakers met with harsh consequences.[25]

The Taliban took control of Kandahar, Afghanistan's second largest city, in 1994. In 1996 they were able to capture Kabul, the country's capital. The Taliban was closely tied to Osama bin Laden and al-Qaeda, the terrorist network responsible for multiple attacks against the United States, including the tragedies of September 11, 2001. When the Taliban refused to surrender bin Laden afterward, the United States and its allies helped Afghanistan's Northern Alliance and other rebel groups remove the Taliban from power.[26]

but Muslims all over the world have rejected this assertion.

On September 11, 2001, Muslim extremists flew two planes into the World Trade Center (Twin Towers) in New York. Another plane flew into the Pentagon, near Washington, D.C. Yet another plane crashed in a Pennsylvania field. It was headed toward another target in Washington, D.C., perhaps the United States Capitol. The plane crashed after the brave passengers fought with the hijackers. Almost three thousand people died that day. They were of every race, nationality, and religious affiliation. It was quickly learned that bin Laden was behind the attacks.

The United States responded to the attacks by overthrowing the Taliban regime in Afghanistan, where bin Laden had been given sanctuary. He and other al-Qaeda leaders went into hiding. Today, bin Laden is believed to be in the mountainous region bordering Afghanistan and Pakistan.

The violent acts of such extremists have made many people fearful of Muslims. They believe Islam teaches Muslims to be violent and hateful, especially toward Americans. The Iraq War, which was launched to remove Saddam Hussein from power in 2003, has created an opportunity for extremists to fight American soldiers and disrupt

American plans for the region. Many Americans interpret the political conflicts as reflections of specific Islamic teachings, instead of interpretations of militants who seek to justify their actions through religion.

"The wholesale destruction of buildings and properties, the bombing and maiming of innocent

In Beijing, China, a Muslim crier, known as a muezzin, calls the hour of the daily prayers from the courtyard of the Niujie Mosque.

men, women and children all are forbidden and detestable acts according to Islam and the Muslims," says one author. "Muslims follow a religion of peace, mercy, and forgiveness, and the vast majority have nothing to do with the violent events some have associated with Muslims. If an individual Muslim were to commit an act of terrorism, the person would be guilty of violating the laws of Islam."[27]

"I . . . know that some Muslims carry out violent acts in Islam's name and use Islam to justify many un-Islamic things," wrote Asma Gull Hasan. "The Islam that I practice is not the one depicted by Osama bin Laden. . . . What Islam is really about is so different from the many misconceptions . . . Islam does not preach violent aggression against one's 'enemies.' In fact, the Qur'an and the core values of American society are strikingly similar."[28]

Muhammad died fourteen centuries ago, but the religion he preached lives on. It is estimated that today more than one billion people in the world are Muslims. Many people believe that most Muslims live in Arab countries. However, less than 20 percent of Muslims are Arabs. Indonesia has the largest Muslim population, followed by Pakistan, Bangladesh, and India. Large Muslim

In Philadelphia, Pennsylvania, Muslim students pray
during school hours.

populations are also found in Africa, Iran, Turkey, China, and the Central Asian republics that formerly were part of the Soviet Union.[29]

Muslim populations are growing in Europe, Canada, and the United States. Many of these Muslims emigrated from other countries. Today, approximately 50 percent of American Muslims were born in the United States. Many are native-born children of immigrants from various countries. Others are African Americans who once were members of the Nation of Islam, a religious group that borrows some elements of Islam. Still other Muslims are converts to Islam from various religious backgrounds.

Brandy Korman grew up in Pennsylvania. She converted to Islam after meeting Osama Abaza. Abaza is an American Muslim who grew up in Egypt and immigrated to the United States. He and Brandy got married and now live in Indiana, where they are college students. Brandy said she converted to Islam because it helped her answer questions she had about God, life after death, and her purpose in life.[30]

In the United States, two famous Muslim converts are rappers Mos Def and Q-Tip. Mos Def took his Shahada, the Muslim declaration of faith, when he was nineteen years old. "You're not [going to] get through life without being worshipful or devoted to something," he said. "You're either devoted to your job, or to your desires. So the best way to spend your life is to try to be devoted to prayer, to Allah."[31]

Eric Shrody, a rap artist also known as Everlast, recalls learning about Islam when he witnessed a friend taking his Shahada. "I remember me being like, 'What is this? I'm white. Can I be here?' It was out of ignorance, you know? 'Cause here in America, Islam is considered a 'Black thing.' And that's when someone pointed out to me, you have no idea how many white Muslims there are in the world."[32]

"To me, Islam is mine," Everlast added. "Allah is the God of all the worlds, and all mankind and all the Al-Amin [worlds/universe]. Islam is my personal relationship with God."[33]

Whether they were born into the religion or converted to it, there are now millions and millions of Muslims in all parts of the world, sharing the same basic set of beliefs and practices. For each and every one of them, the ninth month of the Islamic calendar is a very holy time. When the new moon is sighted, Ramadan begins.

3

The Moon Leads the Way

Many holidays occur at the same time every year. For example, Halloween is always on October 31. Christmas is always on December 25. Thanksgiving is always on the fourth Thursday of November. Some of these holidays are secular, while others are religious. Because the majority of Americans have been Christian since the founding of the nation, important days in the Christian traditions have been part of our common calendar system. They are also recognized as federal holidays.

While many calendars produced today list the holidays of Islam, Judaism, and other faiths, these important days are usually not accommodated through legislation. So to fulfill their religious obligations, Muslims utilize a dating system with historical roots within their tradition. Ramadan is the ninth month of the year as reckoned within the Islamic lunar calendar. This calendar emerged at a time when there were different methods of measuring time in every civilization of the world, from China to India, Africa, the Middle East, Europe, and Central America.

The early followers of Muhammad viewed the revelation of Islam as a momentous event in history. So they assigned year one as the year that Muhammad moved from Mecca, where he was persecuted, to Medina, where he was able to establish a community that secured Islam's future. As Muslims conquered territories outside of Arabia in the seventh and eighth centuries, they established a civilization that used the lunar calendar. It continues to be used by Muslims today for religious purposes. For other purposes, they use the Gregorian calendar, which has become increasingly common to all the world since its creation in 1582 C.E.

For religious purposes, Muslims use the lunar calendar, which follows the phases of the moon.

The lunar calendar follows the stages, or phases, of the moon. The Earth moves around, or orbits, the sun. The moon orbits the Earth. As the moon orbits the Earth from west to east, each night it is illuminated in varying degrees by the sun, depending on the earth's shadow upon it. This is a continuous process, but the process is broken down into eight phases. A new month begins when the moon completes a cycle of these phases and "renews" itself. Throughout most of human history, observing the phases of the moon was the most common way to measure time.

The first phase is the new moon. This is when the moon is not visible in the sky at all. This is because the side of the moon that is not illuminated by the sun is facing Earth. The second phase is waxing crescent. This is when a sliver of the right side of the moon can be seen. Waxing means increasing. So in the next few phases, even more of the moon can be seen in the sky.

The third phase is called the first quarter moon. In this phase, the right half of the moon can be seen. The fourth phase is the waxing gibbous moon. Now, more than half of the moon can be seen. By the fifth phase, or full moon, the entire moon can be seen in the sky.

As the moon continues its orbit, the illumination begins to decrease, or wane. The sixth phase is called the waning gibbous. Much, but not all, of the moon can be seen in the sky. The seventh phase is the last quarter moon. Now, only the left half of the moon can be seen. Next comes the waning crescent. In this eighth and final phase, only a sliver of the left side of the moon can be seen. After the waning crescent, the lunar cycle begins again with the new moon, when the moon is not visible at all. In the Islamic tradition, each month begins on the morning after the newly waxing crescent moon is seen in the evening sky.

It typically takes anywhere from twenty-seven to twenty-nine days for one lunar cycle. This means a lunar month typically is shorter than a month on the common Gregorian calendar, which was designed to correspond to the 365 days of the Earth's revolution around the sun so that dates and seasons could be harmonized.

Ramadan is the ninth month of the Islamic calendar. The English meaning of Ramadan is "the month of great heat." However, because the lunar year is shorter than the solar year by about eleven days, dates in the Islamic calendar occur about eleven days earlier when correlated to the common Gregorian calendar. Thus, the fast (sawm) always

Islamic Calendar

The Islamic calendar begins with the Hegira, Muhammad's flight from Mecca to Medina in A.D. 622 (according to the Gregorian calendar). Although the Islamic calendar is based on the moon instead of the sun, it also has twelve months.[1]

1. Muharram
2. Safar
3. Rabi I
4. Rabi II
5. Jumada I
6. Jumada II
7. Rajab
8. Shaban
9. Ramadan
10. Shawwal
11. Dhu al-Qi'dah[2]
12. Dhu al-Hijjah[3]

begins on the first day of Ramadan, but each year Islamic date will appear about eleven days earlier on the common calendar than it did the year before (for example, on December 14 in one year, and then on December 3 in the following year, and so on.) Thus, Ramadan may not actually be a month of great heat. Over the course of about thirty-three years, Ramadan rotates earlier through the four seasons of winter, fall, summer, and spring continuously.[4]

As with the other eleven months of the Islamic calendar, the month of Ramadan begins the morning after the waxing crescent moon is seen in the sky. According to many Muslims' interpretation of the Qur'an and hadith (sayings of Muhammad), the moon must be seen with the naked eye to confirm the anticipated start of a new month. Many other Muslims believe that the dates of the Islamic calendar can be reliably determined through astronomical study and calculations about the likely visibility of the emerging crescent moon.

Muslims sometimes use a telescope to try to view the thin crescent sliver of a new moon, but they abide by the tradition of witnessing the moon with the naked eye. If it is cloudy, the moon may

In Kuala Lumpur, Malaysia, a local Muslim leader uses a telescope to search for the newly waxing crescent moon.

not be seen, and the month of fasting may be delayed due to the absence of visual confirmation.

In many communities, Muslims climb to the roof of their homes to look for the moon. They know that once they see it, the month of fasting will begin soon. According to tradition, the crescent moon must be seen by at least two reliable witnesses. Muslims rely on astronomical information as well as common sense—they know the previous month has almost reached its conclusion—to predict the start of Ramadan and other months. However, because of variations in interpretation, sightings in one area may not be considered valid in other parts of the world. Also, climatic factors can affect visibility of the new crescent. Thus, the beginning and end of Ramadan may be celebrated on two consecutive days in different countries.[5] There is some debate about whether Muslims should begin Ramadan when the moon is seen by Muslims in other countries, or whether they should wait until after the moon is sighted in their own country.

In 2005, Ramadan began in most of the Middle East on Tuesday, October 4. Official announcements were made by religious leaders and governmental authorities that the crescent moon had been seen the previous evening.[6] In the United States, however, the Islamic Society of North America

(ISNA), a coordinating organization for American Muslims, declared there were no credible sightings of the moon in North America. The society said Ramadan should begin on Wednesday, October 5.

"This is not a major problem," said Rodwan Saleh, president of the Islamic Society of Greater Houston in Texas. "But I would dare to say that there is a small group that will always look for family members overseas to tell them if they have seen the moon."[7]

Mohammed Qarmarul Hasan is the spiritual leader, or imam, of the Al-Noor Society in Houston. He believes Ramadan can begin only when a Muslim sees the moon in his or her hometown. "We have to be very, very careful of who is giving witness," he said. "This is a matter for the entire Muslim community. This is a matter of great importance."[8]

"Every now and then it does get confusing," said Hadi Elmi, a member of the Islamic Education Society. "Normally not, but differences of opinion may arise."[9]

When the waxing crescent moon is sighted, Muslims say a common du'a, or traditional short prayer, addressing the moon as a fellow creation of God: "God is Greater, God is Greater, God is Greater. Praise be to God Who created me and you and Who decreed for you the phases [of the moon] and made you a sign for the universe."[10]

That evening, Muslims eat a small meal and visit the local mosque for special congregational worship that takes place nightly during Ramadan. The holiest month has begun. The next morning, when there is enough light in the sky to tell the difference between a white thread and a black thread, the fasting begins.

Muslims in Kuala Lumpur, Malaysia, buy traditional food for Ramadan at a bazaar.

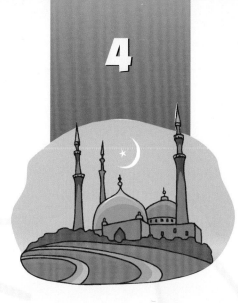

4

Fasting and Prayer

The morning after the crescent moon is seen, the holy month of Ramadan begins. All over the world, Muslims wake up before the sun rises. They eat a small meal, called *sahoor*. When they finish eating, they pray the morning prayer. Often, they sit and read from the Qur'an to increase their spiritual awareness.

By the time the sun rises a little later, the daily fast is under way. According to tradition, despite the modern-day use by Muslims of alarm clocks, the fast begins when there is enough light in the sky to tell the difference between a white thread and a dark thread.

During the daylight hours, Muslims do not eat or drink anything, including water. Smokers may not smoke, and medication routines are adjusted, if possible. As important, Muslims are to refrain

In Saudi Arabia, during the daylight hours of Ramadan, Muslims refrain from eating or drinking, but when the sun goes down, they break their fast with a light snack, or iftar.

from bad thoughts and behaviors, master harmful impulses, and forego entertainment and pleasurable activities, including marital relations. Adherence to these guidelines enables Muslims to focus on God and become more in tune with their own wants and needs, be they physical, emotional, or spiritual. This helps them question their decisions and priorities, and evaluate their path in life. Ramadan is seen by Muslims as a time to renew their faith in God, and to strive to lead a more meaningful life.

When the sun sets for the day, Muslims end the fast with a light snack, called *iftar*. Traditionally, iftar usually includes of a glass of water or milk, and a few dates, which are eaten first to break the fast. A date is the sweet fruit of a desert palm tree.

After iftar, Muslims pray the evening prayer, the fourth of five daily prayers, and then they gather with family and friends for dinner. Wherever they may be, they pray facing toward Mecca, the location of the Ka'bah, a house of worship built by the patriarch Abraham. During Ramadan, Muslims pray more frequently. Each night, they attend special congregational prayers at the mosque. There, a respected community leader called an imam stands in front of the group. He leads the prayers and delivers sermons.

During Ramadan, a special prayer known as

In Paterson, New Jersey, Muslim girls have a traditional iftar of dates to break the fast.

Tarawih is held. Each night, part of the Qur'an is recited sequentially so by the end of the month, the entire Qur'an has been experienced by congregants. In smaller mosques, community members with sufficient knowledge of the Qur'an take turns in the role of imam.[1]

In Taoudenni, Mali, men recite the evening prayer, practicing the second pillar of Islam of praying five times a day.

In 2001, Ramadan took place just weeks after the attacks of September 11th. During Ramadan of that year, Muslims remembered the victims of these attacks in their prayers. "In homes and mosques around our country, many prayers will be uttered for the victims of these horrible attacks and for the families they left behind," wrote Riad Z. Abdelkarim in the *Arab American News*.

He added that prayers would also be said for the Muslims who were victims of hate crimes by fellow Americans in the aftermath of the terrorist attacks. In the United States, approximately one thousand incidents were reported to Muslim civil rights groups. They included harassment, assault, arson, and even murder.[2]

"This Ramadan, American Muslims are most thankful for the support of their neighbors and friends of other faiths," Abdelkarim said. "As our nation turned to war, American Muslims were unequivocal in their support of efforts to bring the perpetrators of the Sept. 11 horrors to justice."[3]

After the Ramadan nightly prayer service, Muslims gather with family or friends for conversation and tea, or to eat a modest dinner if they did not dine earlier. It probably is similar to the meal that Favel Hussain al-Mousawi, of Baghdad, and his family enjoyed during one night of Ramadan in 2005. Al-Mousawi and his wife ate yogurt, stuffed grape leaves, and lamb stew. Joining them in the meal were their four grown sons and their two daughters.

"The whole family is together," said al-Mousawi's daughter Jameela. "It's really nice. And

In Dhaka, Bangladesh, people break their fast with this colorful dish garnished with tomatoes, cucumbers, and chili peppers.

whoever is angry at someone forgets his anger and starts anew."[4]

After eating, the al-Mousawi family usually watches Ramadan quiz shows on television. Then they go to bed so that they will be able to get up early the next morning for sahoor. They and their neighbors will be awakened by a teenager who walks the street banging a drum. "Wake up," the teen shouts. "You who are fasting, wake up. It's time for suhoor [sic]." The drummer later explains that some people do not have clocks to wake them, so they are grateful to the teen for letting them know when it is time to get up.[5]

Fasting can be very difficult, especially for those who are not in good health. Thus, sick and elderly people are not required to fast. Nor are young children, pregnant women, and nursing mothers. Travelers are also exempt from fasting. However, they are expected to make up the fast days after they return home.

Ramadan also can be challenging for Muslim athletes, particularly teenage ones. Zohayr Jaffer plays football at a high school in Pennsylvania. In 2005, Ramadan occurred during football season. While teammates gulped water after workouts, Jaffer simply wiped his face with the end of his shirt.[6]

Jaffer said it was hard to not drink anything during or after practice. However, he said he did not want any special treatment. His coach did give Jaffer permission to eat a sandwich during evening games to break the fast after sunset. The coach also gave Jaffer time to pray.[7]

A Muslim doctor said athletes who fast during Ramadan and then participate in physical activities before breaking the fast may become dehydrated. They also may experience other problems, such as muscle cramping. This doctor advises Muslim athletes to "not play as intensely" when they are fasting.[8]

Some athletes have learned how to cope, however. Hakeem Olajuwon was a professional basketball player for almost two decades. He was named one of the fifty greatest National Basketball Association (NBA) players ever. He is also a devout Muslim. To be devout means to closely follow all the teachings and duties of a religion. During Ramadan, Olajuwon continued to compete. He developed the habit of eating exactly seven dates and drinking a gallon of water for his sahoor. This meal lasted him until after sunset.[9]

"I find myself full of energy, explosive," he said. "And when I break the fast at sunset, the taste of water is so precious . . . You feel so privileged, because [Ramadan] is a month of mercy, forgiveness, getting closer to God."[10]

Ramadan can be difficult, but most Muslims joyfully anticipate its arrival. They recognize its significance. Each Muslim decides for himself or

In Dearborn, Michigan, this woman cooks her family's Ramadan feast. She embraces Western culture, but she and her family fast during Ramadan.

herself how to appropriately fulfill religious duties in relation to events and commitments in life. Even Muslims who are not particularly devout sometimes fast during Ramadan.

Anni Shamim, who lives in Connecticut, said she is not a very observant Muslim. But during the 2005 Ramadan, she fasted for a few days. "Tomorrow when I drive in to the center of town to mail a letter . . . nobody will have a clue that I am fasting," she said. "None of the shops will be offering complimentary copies of timetables listing the changing daily times for starting and breaking each fast . . . But I'm trying to do my part in bringing a Muslim tradition into America's cultural mix and inviting everyone to celebrate with me. In a growingly hostile world, Muslim children need a sense of normalcy regarding their heritage."[11]

"Fasting is not just about giving up food or drink," said Haajira Cheema, a Muslim teenager who lives in Oklahoma. "It's really just a way of remembering unfortunate people who do not have what you have. It's a time in which you truly feel thankful for what God has given you."[12]

She added, "Knowing that I am fasting with millions of Muslims all over the world is a very powerful feeling. It is the feeling of unity and completeness that makes Ramadan such a moving and extraordinary experience."[13]

Seher Chowdhry is a Muslim who wrote about Ramadan for a local newspaper in Virginia. "A true fast requires one to abandon all negative behaviors while devoting time to religious acts," Chowdhry wrote. "Giving charity to the poor, helping out those in need, worshiping God, not fighting or arguing, and abandoning all sorts of permissible pleasures contributes to a good fast, a fast one keeps for God."[14]

Inayat Bunglawala works at the Muslim Council of Britain. He remembers that when he was a child, he would wake up during Ramadan "in the early hours for my predawn meal, at the height of the long summer days, in the fervent expectation that this time I would try and complete the whole day's fast." He added, "With the passing of each successive Ramadan, the Muslim character ought to develop, mature, and enhance."[15]

"Ramadan should . . . be seen as an opportunity to renew and strengthen oneself with the challenge being not only to curb one's appetite for basic animal needs but to also rein in negative emotional conditions, especially anger, greed, intolerance, arrogance, and dishonesty," he said.[16]

During Ramadan, most schools in Fairfax County, Virginia, allow Muslim students to avoid the cafeteria at lunchtime. Instead, they can read in the library, or go to another part of the school. The students are also excused from activities such as running the mile during physical education class.

Sabrina Aman, a student at a Fairfax County high school, said fasting is not just about avoiding food and drink. It is also about having a clean heart and becoming closer to God. She said that during Ramadan, her non-Muslim friends sometimes complain about their teachers and friends. When this happens, Aman says to herself, "Ana sa'imah." In Arabic, this means, "I am fasting," indicating that she does not wish to participate in the discussion. Then, she leaves the room.[17]

Sometimes, dealing with other people is the most trying aspect of Ramadan. Uzma Khan is a student in North Carolina. She remembers what happened during the Ramadan of her seventh-grade year. A group of boys asked her what her favorite food was. She told them it was popcorn. The next day, the boys brought popcorn to school to tempt her. "It was really crazy," she said.[18]

In many countries with large Muslim populations, people work only half days during the month of Ramadan, or business hours are extended into the night. This schedule allows Muslims time to alter their sleep patterns, save energy, and focus on prayers and other acts of worship that they believe will be rewarded by God even more than at other times of the year. While employers in the United States sometimes try to accommodate some of the religious needs of their employees, including Muslims, business practices do not uniformly shift as they do in other countries. Depending on the nature of their jobs, American Muslims sometimes adjust their personal work schedules and vacation times to enable them to enjoy Ramadan without affecting their overall performance.

"Ramadan is very challenging—not just because you cannot eat but also because, if you are in a non-Islamic country, you don't have the luxury of staying home and sleeping in," said author Asma Gull Hasan. She joked, "Those of us in law school are forced to sleep in class instead!"[19]

"It gets harder to study during Ramadan because you're so busy" fasting and praying, said Saba Syed, who is a student at the University of Houston. "If you can [manage a busy schedule] during this month, you can do it for the rest of the year."[20]

The entire month of Ramadan is very special. But one night holds particular significance. It is called Laylat al-Qadar, or Night of Power. This is usually toward the end of the month, on one of the odd-numbered nights. It commemorates the night when the angel Gabriel gave the first revelation to the prophet Muhammad in 610 c.e. In Morocco, Muslim youths set off fireworks in the streets to celebrate.

On the twenty-seventh night of Ramadan, called Laylat al-Qadar, or the Night of Power, Muslims pray in the Al-Aqsa Mosque in Jerusalem, Israel.

During the Night of Power, many Muslims stay up all night praying to God, usually at the mosque.[21] Many believe that those who do so are forgiven for all of their previous sins, since they spend the night in repentance and spiritual renewal. Muslims believe that sacrifice and penance are more valued by God during Ramadan than at any other time of the year.[22] "In Ramadan, the doors of paradise are opened and the doors of hell are closed and the devils are chained," said Shaykh al-Qaradawi, an Egyptian imam based in Qatar.[23]

During the final ten days of Ramadan, a few Muslims also engage in I'tikaf, or retreat. During this time, they live and study in the prayer area of their mosque. They do not leave unless it is for an emergency or to bathe and change clothes.[24]

The final days of the ninth month are very busy. Muslim families prepare special meals that they will eat when Ramadan ends. They buy new clothes to wear to the special congregational prayer held at the conclusion of the month. They purchase gifts for family members, and make plans to spend time with each other. They clean the house to prepare to receive many visitors.

The month of Ramadan ends just as it begins. Muslims sight the crescent that becomes visible after the birth of the new moon. This sighting means that Ramadan has ended and the tenth month has begun. If the moon cannot be seen because of clouds, the end of Ramadan is delayed for another day.

The tenth month in Islam is called *Shawwal.* This means "the month of hunting." The first three days of the month are set aside for the Festival of Fast Breaking, or 'Id al Fitr. Ramadan has ended; let the party begin.

In Austin, Texas, Turkish dancers celebrate 'Id al Fitr in the End of Ramadan Festival. All faiths are welcome to enjoy the food, dancing, and events.

5

'Id al Fitr: Festival of Fast Breaking

s a child, Bushra Malik grew more and more excited as the days of Ramadan passed. She knew that soon, the night would come when the waxing crescent moon would be visible in the sky. That night would be the last night of Ramadan. The next morning's sunrise would usher in the tenth month. This month begins with the Festival of Fast Breaking, or 'Id al Fitr. "Everyone would wait to hear about the sighting of the moon to announce 'Id day," Malik recalls.[1]

In many countries, the sighting of the moon is officially announced. Much like people in the United States count down to midnight on New Year's Eve, Muslims await word on whether the moon has been seen. If it is cloudy, the end of Ramadan may be delayed.

During the last night or two of Ramadan, many Muslims in countries other than the United States keep their radios or televisions on constantly in the evenings. They are listening for official word of the crescent moon's sighting. In Qatar, the sighting of the moon is also announced by blowing sirens or firing cannonballs.[2] In the United States, Muslims call their local mosques or check various Web sites that post announcements about the holiday.

The word "'Id," which is also spelled "Eid," means recurring happiness. 'Id celebrates the happiness Muslims feel about completing Ramadan. 'Id also is a time of hope for a new life filled with blessings.[3]

Once the crescent moon is sighted, many Muslim families rush to the shops for last-minute purchases of food and presents. Women also gather together in a home or beauty salon for henna painting. Henna is a reddish-brown dye that comes from the leaves of the henna plant. Using henna to paint intricate designs on the body is an

In London, England, two girls read Eid cards they received for 'Id al-Fitr. Eid, or 'Id, means "recurring happiness" and like Ramadan, it begins with the sighting of the waxing crescent moon.

ancient custom. It is similar to tattooing, but it is not permanent. Designs last for several weeks before fading.

During Ramadan, Muslim women do not adorn themselves with perfume, makeup, or henna. But on "henna night," they paint elaborate designs on their fingertips and palms, and soles of their feet. They are preparing to look their best for the 'Id service at the mosque.[4]

In many countries, 'Id is a national holiday. Muslims are expected to give a special donation called a Sadaqat al-Fitr, or Charity of the Fast Breaking. These donations allow the mosque to arrange meals for the poor. Muslims usually give the equivalent of the cost of one meal per person, multiplied by the number of people in the house.[5]

This donation must be paid no later than dawn on 'Id day. However, Muslims often pay a few days early so that the money can be used to help the poor purchase food and clothing for the holiday celebration.[6]

'Id morning typically begins with a special light, sweet snack. As a child, Bushra Malik traditionally ate a sweet vermicelli noodle pudding called *kheer*.[7] Muslims do not worry about such a light meal after a month of fasting. They know that the 'Id celebration involves a feast of foods. First,

In Marshfield, Wisconsin, this girl has her hands painted with henna to look her best in celebration of 'Id al-Fitr.

however, they go to the mosque for a special prayer service.

"We would all have new clothes to wear for 'Id day," Malik recalls of her childhood. "It was a mad rush in our house as everyone would be getting ready to go to the mosque for special [Id] prayers followed by a sermon."[8]

Muslims take great care in getting ready for the 'Id prayer service. It is important that each family member bathes and then dresses in new clothes. If the clothes cannot be new, they must be very clean. Muslim men usually wear white clothes. White symbolizes purity and dignity.[9] They also wear perfume or incense. Islamic teachings emphasize that people should be clean and presentable, which includes smelling good.[10]

In some cultures, Muslim women dress in their fanciest new outfits, and adorn themselves with many bangle bracelets and other jewelry. Asma Gull Hasan is from Pakistan. She recalls an 'Id service she attended at a mosque in New York. She wore embroidered pants with a long tunic. This ethnic dress is called *shalwar-kameez*. "When Eid finally comes," she said, "the excitement of a holiday is joined by the excitement of returning to a normal daily routine."[11]

In Dhaka, Bangladesh, a girl participates in a henna competition. After a month of refraining from using perfume, makeup, or henna, women adorn their hands and feet with intricate designs for 'Id al-Fitr.

In Dhaka, Bangladesh, women shop for new clothes.

With everyone looking and smelling their best, it is now time for the 'Id service. Many mosques have separate entrances for men and women. The prayer area must remain clean, so the men and women remove their shoes upon entering the mosque. Many mosques have cubbies for the shoes.[12]

The men gather on one side; the women on the other. They recite prayers while facing toward Mecca. They also recite the prayers in unison, following the imam's movements. Together, Muslims stand and bow. They also prostrate themselves. This is when they kneel on the floor and touch their forehead to the ground. Their arms are at their sides, and their palms are against the carpet.[15] This position demonstrates submission to God. Muslims say, "Glory be to God, the Most High."

The 'Id service is an exciting jumble of images and sounds. "All the women are together, dressed in their finest clothes and wearing multiple bracelets," said Bushra Malik. "You can hear the collective jingling of the bangles every time the women raise their hands to recite, 'Allaahu Akbar [God is great].'"[16]

The 'Id prayer is followed by the *khutba*, or sermon. Then, Muslims recite a prayer asking for forgiveness, mercy, and help from God for Muslims

Clothing

The Qur'an emphasizes modesty in dress, which means that Muslims must wear clothing that hides their bodies and is not too bright. That is why many devout Muslims, regardless of gender, are usually covered from head to toe and frequently wear earth tones such as green, blue, and gray, as well as black and white.[13]

When Muslims travel to Mecca, the pilgrimage known as hajj, they must wear special clothing. The men wear two white sheets, while the women wear a modest white dress and are not allowed to wear gloves or veils. This way, each individual looks like the others, and are all equal in the eyes of God. Only the virtue and devotion to their faith that lies within them makes them different from each other.[14]

around the world. At this time, it is customary for Muslims to embrace the person sitting on either side of them, men hugging men and women hugging women.[17] Family members also embrace each other.

In many Muslim countries, such as Qatar in the Arabian Gulf, Muslims gather in a special designated open space called a *musalla*, rather than at a mosque. The musalla provides a much larger space for thousands of Muslims to gather for the 'Id prayer. After the sermon is completed, Muslims greet one another and then make plans for the rest of the day.[18]

When the praying ends, the celebrations begin. Many Muslims hold lavish feasts in their homes. The first day of 'Id is often devoted to family members. Visits with friends and neighbors come during the next two days of the holiday.

During the get-togethers, Muslims sometimes exchange gifts. Children receive gifts as well as small amounts of money. This money is called *idiyah*. Later, children often walk along the streets singing 'Id songs. The practice is similar to Christmas caroling. Neighbors often reward the singing children with idiyah.

'Id gatherings can be quite festive. Drinking and dancing are not part of the festivities. Many

Muslims gather at one family home for sweet foods and drinks such as Sekanjabin, a beverage made from mint. Then, they travel to the home of the oldest or wealthiest member of the family. There, they eat lunch. Among Arab Muslims, a typical meal consists of boiled lamb and rice, while African-American Muslims might serve roast turkey. In some families, men and women eat separately, while in others they intermix.

Despite the cultural diversity among Muslims, an abundance of food is common. There is usually so much food that Muslims offer baskets of sweets and pastries to their neighbors. They make plans to meet during the next day or so for lunch, dinner, afternoon tea, or coffee.[19]

"My Eids, starting at about age 12, were about planning [and] logistics," wrote Reshma Memom Yaqub. "I would do anything it took to accomplish my Eid goal: getting me and my two closest friends, Farin and Sajeela, in the same place."[20]

"We'd compare notes on what mosque service our parents would attend the next day, and which of their friends they would visit afterward—in which order, at which times, with what range of variables."[21]

Sometimes, Reshma and her friends actually managed to attend the same mosque service. "If we

In Austin, Texas, children come face to face with camels at the End of Ramadan Festival.

knew the chance of meeting up again was dismal, we swapped presents right from our car trunks. We did so as [quickly and quietly] as possible, given that we were surrounded by other friends with whom our junior high school budgets (and priorities) did not allow Eid gift exchanges."[22]

Some Muslim families eat the 'Id meal at their favorite restaurant. Many restaurants in Muslim countries are closed during Ramadan. When 'Id day arrives, they come alive.

Many towns hold lively street festivals to celebrate 'Id. The festivals feature food, carnival rides, and booths for henna painting. In Bahrain, the 'Id festival features donkey rides. The donkeys have been painted with henna.[23]

Many towns in the United States also hold 'Id festivals. Approximately one thousand people attended an 'Id festival in Sterling, Virginia, in 2005. The festival was sponsored by the All Dulles Area Muslim Society Center. It featured food, recordings of Qur'an readings, and booths displaying perfumed oils from the Persian Gulf. Activities for children at such carnivals include rides, dunk tanks, the "moon bounce," sack races, and other games.

Riyad Shamma of Cincinnati came with his family to the Virginia 'Id festival. Shamma was in town visiting with relatives. "This is a celebration of remembering God and joyous times," he said of 'Id. "You want to make it a special day for the kids."[24]

Many people believe it is important to share that feeling with everyone, Muslim and non-Muslim alike. "How great it would be to weave . . . the holiday of 'Id into the fabric of American . . . culture," said Anni Shamim. "How wonderful it would be to see banners and streamers reading Happy 'Id on the shop fronts [and hold festivals] . . . where all are welcome to have their hands henna painted, try on a hundred colors of glittering glass bangles, eat cheap vendor food, and celebrate with the community."[25]

In January 1998, President William Clinton became the first United States leader to publicly wish the Muslim community a happy 'Id al Fitr. "It's a time for rejoicing and celebration, a time of family and community," he said in a videotaped broadcast. "It is also a time for reflection and for recommitting ourselves to the values of tolerance, mutual respect, and understanding. In a world where many Muslims suffer the terrible consequences of war, poverty, and unrest, we must renew our efforts to resolve conflicts and remove the causes of strife."[26]

Iraqi women shop at a local bazaar in preparation for Ramadan.

He added, "We can build a better future—one of cooperation, understanding, and compassion—for ourselves and for generations to come . . . As the new moon ushers in this holy celebration, let me say to all who follow the faith of Islam: As-Salaamu alaykum. May peace be with you and may God grant you health and prosperity, now and in the years ahead."[27]

Two years later, President Clinton invited American Muslim leaders to attend an 'Id al Fitr reception at the White House. He became the first president in office to meet with American Muslim leaders. "Too many Americans still know too little about Islam," Clinton said, "now practiced by one of every four people."[28]

Today, awareness about Islam has increased. Many schools throughout the United States offer excused absences or even holidays for 'Id. School officials are also more sensitive to the needs of students during Ramadan. Additionally, throughout the year, Friday prayer services are held in the United States Capitol for Muslims who are federal employees. In 2001, the United States Post Office issued a stamp to commemorate the 'Id holiday.

Awareness has increased. But so, too, have fears and misconceptions about the religion of Islam.

Lance Cpl. David Bauman, 1st Battalion, 6th Marines, holds a Kurdish baby during the festivities of 'Id al Fitr in 1997, in the Middle East.

Many non-Muslims believe that Islam promotes terror and violence. Fears and misconceptions run high on the other side, as well. Many Muslims around the world believe that Westerners, particularly Americans, are self-righteous and mainly driven by money. International relations are very complex, and often fuel misconceptions and fears among various groups of people.

The September 2001 terrorist attacks, and the American military response that followed them, have heightened emotions and raised the possibility of long-term conflict. People now face the challenge of distinguishing between authentic religious traditions and extremist interpretations by some, and between religious concepts and specific political ideas. It is critical to understand Islam as a worldwide faith that has been practiced for many centuries in many parts of the world, and that the vast majority of Muslims throughout the world seek a better future for all of humanity.

In Austin, Texas, girls socialize at the End of Ramadan Festival. About seven million Muslims from all different races and backgrounds live in the United States.

6

Challenges and Opportunities

More than one billion people in the world are Muslims. Of that number, approximately seven million live in the United States. Many Muslims are immigrants to this country. Or, they are the children of immigrants. Other Muslims living in the United States are converts to Islam.

"I'm not an American kid who goes out and drinks," said Haider Javed, a youth coordinator for an Islamic center in California. "I'm not entirely

In Illinois, Principal Habeeb Quadri leads his students in prayer for the start of Ramadan.

Pakistani either. But I am thoroughly Muslim. I feel comfortable at the Islamic center, like this is where I actually belong."[1]

He glanced around at the other Muslims in the center. Then he said, "I'm looking at one Pakistani, one white guy, one Palestinian, one African-American guy. They're just standing around, talking. That alone makes me believe America is the perfect place for Islam."[2]

The Muslim population in the United States is a mixture of races and ethnic backgrounds. This group of diverse people has learned to look past their differences and unite in their common bond: the religion of Islam. They are trying to forge a bond between other religious groups as well.

"Islam is one of the world's great religions," said Bernard Lewis, a professor at Princeton University. "It has brought comfort and peace of mind to countless millions of men and women. It has given dignity and meaning to drab and impoverished lives . . . But Islam, like other religions, has also known periods when it inspired in some followers a mood of hatred and violence."[3]

Adeed Dawisha, a Muslim professor at Miami University, said some Muslims cite verses from the Qur'an to try to justify violence during Ramadan.

In Union City, New Jersey, a fourteen-year-old
Muslim and a sixteen-year-old Jew laugh and talk at
the Palisades Emergency Residence Corporation, a
homeless shelter. They are two of about twenty
Muslim and Jewish girls working together to help
establish a shelter for homeless families.

"To people like that, who are moved basically by their faith, you can understand that it is in a month where faith is paramount, that they basically do their work," he said.[4]

Adding to the confusion is that in parts of Baghdad, extremists use mosques as headquarters to hide their activities. Shortly before Ramadan of 2004, United States soldiers and Iraqi forces raided seven mosques. Their purpose was to prevent attacks during the upcoming holy month. United States officials wanted to be respectful of Islam and Muslim houses of worship. However, they also wanted to save lives.[5]

With globalization, terrorism, and war, can developed Western nations and underdeveloped countries, such as those in the Middle East, ever establish mutual respect and learn to cooperate more effectively for a brighter shared future? Worldwide, the task seems overwhelming, even impossible. But in individual neighborhoods, in cities and towns all over, progress is being made. Little by little, people of many faiths and cultures are reaching out, trying to understand and accept each other. In particular, many Muslims and non-Muslims are working to build bridges.

Gina Gallagher of Virginia, is not Muslim. But in 2005, she attended an 'Id festival in Sterling,

A press photo from the documentary *Three Faiths, One God: Judaism, Christianity, Islam,* shows a Muslim volunteer from the Interfaith Youth Core in Chicago tutoring an immigrant student. The documentary explores the practices and beliefs shared by the three religions as well as the historic conflicts among them and the steps people are taking toward reconciliation.

Virginia. It was the second year she had attended the event. Gallagher said the previous year, she had been surprised to learn she had some things in common with the Muslim women. "A lot of people look at the women with the head-scarves and they can't relate," Gallagher said. "You look at a woman like that and you're like, 'I don't have anything in common with her.' And then you sit down, you eat, you realize you all have the same problems."[6]

"In this society, everybody has to learn to live together," said Zohra Shrief, a Muslim from Pakistan who now also lives in Virginia. "If I isolate myself from the [American] society, it's my loss."[7]

Bushra Malik recalls that after September 11, 2001, Muslim friends warned her against wearing her hijab, or Muslim dress, in public. They were afraid she would be a target of harassment or even violence. "But I felt confident in my faith and God, and by the grace of God, I have not suffered any confrontation," she said. "Maybe it is the metropolitan area that we live in. It is so diverse, and people have been educated with awareness."[8]

Awareness, acceptance, faith, trust, respect. These words are integral to any faith, and to relationships among all people. The month of

A father and his two young daughters show their American pride as they march in the Muslim Day Parade in New York.

Ramadan is a holy time, and the Id' al Fitr holiday is a celebration of that holiness. For Muslims, Ramadan is the ideal time to cultivate these qualities to become constructive members of society.

Give!

Charitable giving is one of the pillars of the Islam religion. Muslims who have a certain standard of living and possess a surplus of wealth are required each year to give money, goods, or property to the less fortunate. Or, they may make donations to benefit the entire Muslim community.

Even if you are not Muslim, you can observe this important Ramadan tradition with a collection jar.

1 Find an empty container with a lid that fits snugly. (A large coffee can works well.) With an adult's help, make a slit in the center of the lid so that money can be placed inside.

2 Cover the container with black construction paper, and then use white crayons or paint to decorate the paper with moons and stars. Ask your teacher if you can bring the container to school so that classmates can also participate.

3 Every day for one month, you and your classmates could bring spare change to school to put into the container. At the end of the month, donate the money to a community or school group.

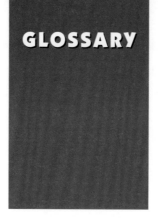

GLOSSARY

chaste—Pure in thoughts and actions.

fast—To not eat or drink for a certain period of time and for a specific reason.

henna—Reddish-brown dye that comes from the leaves of the henna plant. Using henna to paint intricate designs on the body is an ancient custom.

integral—Essential to completeness.

Mecca—The birth place of Muhammad.

mosque—A Muslim house of worship.

Muhammad—The final prophet of God, according to Islam.

Muslims—Followers of the religion known as Islam, literally translated as "those who submit to God."

persecuted—To be harassed or threatened for religious beliefs, sexual identity, or other reasons.

prostrate—A position of submission in which a person kneels on the floor with forehead touching the ground. Palms are on the ground in front of them.

Qur'an—The Islamic holy book believed to be the Word of God delivered to Muhammad.

Ramadan—The ninth and most holy month of the Islamic calendar, during which Muslims pray and fast.

revelation—A communication from a divine being.

waning—Decreasing.

waxing—Increasing.

CHAPTER NOTES

◈ Chapter 1. Praying, Fasting, Celebrating

1. Personal e-mail and telephone interview with Bushra Malik, December 2005.
2. Ibid.
3. Ibid.

◈ Chapter 2. Muhammad: God's Final Prophet

1. "The Prophet," *The Holiday Spot*, n.d., <http://www.theholidayspot.com/ramadan/prophet.htm> (September 28, 2006); Muhammad Hamidullah, "The Prophet of Islam - His Biography," USC-MSA Compendium of Muslim Texts, n.d., <http://www.usc.edu/dept/MSA/fundamentals/prophet/profbio.html> (September 28, 2006).
2. Ibid.
3. "The Afterlife: The Resurrection," *IslamOnline.net*, August 14, 2003, <http://www.islamonline.net/english/introducingislam/Belief/Afterlife/article01.shtml> (September 19, 2006).
4. "Muslim Beliefs about the Afterlife," *ReligionFacts*, February 14, 2005, <http://www.religionfacts.com/islam/beliefs/afterlife.htm> (September 19, 2006).
5. "Description in the Qur'an of Paradise," *Madrasah In'aamiyyah, Camperdown*, April 4, 2006, <http://www.alinaam.org.za/library/paradise1.htm> (September 19, 2006).
6. "Muslim Beliefs about the Afterlife."

7. "The Noble Qur'an," *USC-MSA Compendium of Muslim Texts*, n.d., <http://www.usc.edu/dept/MSA/quran/> (September 28, 2006).

8. "Ismaili Imamat," *Aga Khan Development Network*, n.d., <http://www.akdn.org/imamat/imamat.html> (October 30, 2006).

9. Matthew S. Gordon, *Islam* (New York: Oxford University Press, 2002), pp. 49, 61; Hamidullah.

10. I. A. Ibrahim, ed., *A Brief Illustrated Guide to Understanding Islam* (Houston: Darussalam Publishers and Distributors, 1997), p. 5.

11. Gordon, p. 38.

12. Ibid., p. 39.

13. Yahiya Emerick, *The Complete Idiot's Guide to Understanding Islam* (Indianapolis: Alpha Books, 2002), p. 149.

14. Eric M. Meyers, "Abraham," *World Book Encyclopedia*, Vol. 1, 2005, pp. 16–17.

15. Richard C. Martin, "Kaaba," *World Book Encyclopedia*, Vol. 11, 2005, p. 208.

16. Asma Gull Hasan, *Why I am a Muslim: An American Odyssey* (London: Element, an imprint of Harper Collins Publishers, 2004), pp. 91–92.

17. Ibrahim, p. 52.

18. Charles S. J. White, "Hinduism," *World Book Encyclopedia*, Vol. 9, 2005, p. 236.

19. Mark Juergensmeyer, "Polytheism," *World Book Encyclopedia*, Vol. 15, 2005, pp. 651–2.

20. Mark Juergensmeyer, "Pantheism," *World Book Encyclopedia*, Vol. 15, 2005, p. 131.

21. Gull Hasan, p. ix.

22. Ibrahim, p. 61.

23. "Responsibility for the Terrorist Atrocities in the United States, 11 September 2001—An Updated

Account," *10 Downing Street*, n.d., <http://www.number-10.gov.uk/output/page3682.asp> (September 28, 2006); Charles Paul Freund, "2001 Nights: The End of the Orientalist Critique," *Reason online*, December 2001 <http://www.reason.com/0112/cr.cf.2001.shtml> (September 28, 2006).

24. Abraham Marcus, "Taliban," *World Book Encyclopedia*, Vol. 19, 2005, p. 19.

25. Ibid.

26. Ibid., pp. 19–20.

27. Ibrahim, p. 61.

28. Gull Hasan, pp. xii–xiv.

29. Gordon, p. 9.

30. Charmi Keranen, "Couple eager to focus on duty to God at Ramadan," *South Bend Tribune*, September 29, 2005, Faith section.

31. Ali Asadullah, "You're Gonna Serve Somebody," *Beliefnet*, 2006, <http://www.beliefnet.com/story/75/story_7526_1.html> (September 28, 2006).

32. Adisa Banjoko, "Being Muslim One Day at a Time: An interview with Everlast," n.d., <http://www.uga.edu/islam/everlast_banjoko.html> (September 28, 2006).

33. Ibid.

◆ Chapter 3. **The Moon Leads the Way**

1. Irene Cockroft, "Calendar," *World Book Encyclopedia*, Vol. 3, 2005, p. 29.

2. "The Twelve Months of the Islamic Calendar," *Ramadan-Islam.org*, 2003, <http://www.ramadan-islam.org/ramadan/12months.html> (September 20, 2006).

3. Ibid.

4. "We wish you all a blessed Ramadan," *The Arab American News*, October 22, 2004.

5. "We wish you all a blessed Ramadan," *The Arab American News*, October 16, 2004.

6. Tara Dooley, "Ramadan starts today in Mideast, but not here," *Houston Chronicle*, October 4, 2005.

7. Ibid.

8. Ibid.

9. Ibid.

10. Yahiya Emerick, *The Complete Idiot's Guide to Understanding Islam* (Indianapolis: Alpha Books, 2002), p. 146.

◆ Chapter 4. Fasting and Prayer

1. John Esposito, *What Everyone Needs to Know About Islam* (New York: Oxford University Press, 2002), p. 35.

2. Riad Z. Abdelkarim, "Ramadan: Reflecting on Sept. 11 and Beyond," *Arab American News*, November 23, 2001, p. 10.

3. Ibid.

4. Anne Garrels reporting, "Profile: Postcard from Baghdad; Observing Ramadan," transcript from National Public Radio Show *Morning Edition*, October 27, 2005.

5. Ibid.

6. Romy Varghese, "Muslim athletes balancing spirituality with sports. During Ramadan, they must fast regardless of demands on the body," *Allentown Morning Call*, October 16, 2005.

7. Ibid.

8. Ibid.

9. Andrew Mikula, "Ramadan runner—nutrition becomes challenge during fast," *Daytona Beach News-Journal*, October 18, 2005.

10. Deborah Caldwell, "Hakeem Olajuwon: A Ramadan Interview," *Beliefnet,* 2006, <http://belief.net/story/55/story_5556_1.html> (September 28, 2006).

11. Anni Shamim, "Commentary: Celebrating and sharing Ramadan," transcript from National Public Radio Show *All Things Considered,* October 13, 2005.

12. Haajira Cheema, "Muslims the world over prepare to fast and celebrate Ramadan," *Tulsa World,* September 30, 2005.

13. Ibid.

14. Seher Chowdhry, "Ramadan: A First Person Account," *Centre View,* October 27–November 2, 2005, p. 4.

15. "Reflections on Ramadan," *BBC News, UK Edition,* November 25, 2003, <http://news.bbc.co.uk/2/hi/uk_news/3233518.stm> (September 28, 2006).

16. Ibid.

17. Nashiah Ahmad, "Schools adapting to Muslim holy month," *Education Week,* November 27, 2002, vol. 2, no. 13.

18. Ibid.

19. Asma Gull Hasan, *Why I am a Muslim: An American Odyssey* (London: Element, an imprint of Harper Collins Publishers, 2004), p. 20.

20. Julie Afonso, "UH Muslims observe Ramadan," *The Daily Cougar online,* October 18, 2005, Volume 71, No. 36, <http://www.stp.uh.edu/vol71/36/news/news4.html> (September 28, 2006).

21. Yahiya Emerick, *The Complete Idiot's Guide to Understanding Islam* (Indianapolis: Alpha Books, 2002), p. 148.

22. Noah Adams, "Celebration: Ramadan in Michigan," transcript from National Public Radio Special, November 10, 2004.

23. "Near/Middle East: Round-up for Friday sermons," *BBC Monitoring Middle East*, September 30, 2005, <www.elibrary.bigchalk.com> (October 4, 2005).

24. Emerick, p. 148.

◆ Chapter 5. 'Id al Fitr: Festival of Fast Breaking

1. Personal interview with Bushra Malik, December 2005.

2. Rachel Hajar, "Recurring Happiness—Qatar Celebrates Eid al-Fitr," *The World & I*, January 1, 2000, Vol. 15.

3. Ibid.

4. Ibid.

5. Yahiya Emerick, *The Complete Idiot's Guide to Understanding Islam* (Indianapolis: Alpha Books, 2002), p. 148.

6. Excerpt from *Everyday Fiqh* by Abdul Aziz Kamal, reprinted on "Sadaqah Fitr," or Charity at the time of Fitr, n.d., <www.muslim-canada.org/IDALFITR.html> (September 28, 2006).

7. Personal interview with Bushra Malik, December 2005.

8. Ibid.

9. "Id Fiesta," *The Holiday Spot*, n.d., <http://www.theholidayspot.com/ramadan/fiesta.htm> (September 28, 2006).

10. Hajar.

11. Asma Gull Hasan, *Why I am a Muslim: An American Odyssey* (London: Element, an imprint of Harper Collins Publishers, 2004), p. 20.

12. Ibid, p. 21.

13. Christine Huda Dodge, "Islamic Clothing," *About.Islam*, n.d., <http://islam.about.com/library/weekly/aa020900a.htm> (September 20, 2006).

14. Carolyn Ruff, "Exploring Islam," *Washingtonpost.com*, May 13, 1998, <http://www.founders.howard.edu/islamwp/islamwp1.htm> (September 20, 2006).

15. Ibid.

16. Personal interview with Bushra Malik, December 2005.

17. "Eid ul-Fitr," *Answers.com*, 2006, <http://www.answers.com/eid%20ul-fitr> (September 28, 2006).

18. Hajar.

19. Ibid.

20. Reshma Memon Yaqub, "The Eid Miracle; What keeps friends together through that obstacle course called life," *The Washington Post Magazine*, November 24, 2005, p. 28.

21. Ibid.

22. Ibid.

23. Catherine Cartwright-Jones, "Henna traditions for the end of Ramadan," *The Encyclopedia of Henna*, 2003, <http://www.hennapage.com/henna/encyclopedia/ramadan/> (September 28, 2006).

24. Arianne Aryanpur, "For Muslims, the Fasting Begins—Festival at Center in Sterling Marks End of Ramadan," *The Washington Post*, November 10, 2005, final edition, Prince William Extra.

25. Anni Shamim, "Commentary: Celebrating and sharing Ramadan," transcript from National Public Radio Show *All Things Considered*, October 13, 2005.

26. "Videotaped remarks by the president on the occasion of Id al Fitr," Press Release, Office of the

Press Secretary, The White House, January 29, 1998.

27. Ibid.

28. Asma Gull Hasan, *American Muslims: The New Generation* (New York: Continuum, 2002), p. 153.

❖ Chapter 6. Challenges and Opportunities

1. Lorraine Ali, "A New Welcoming Spirit in the Mosque," *Newsweek*, Vol. 146, August 29–September 5, 2005, p. 53.

2. Ibid.

3. "Comparative Religion Quotations File: Focusing on Islamism," The Lair of Fang-Face DreamWeaver, n.d., <http://www.angelfire.com/scifi/dreamweaver/quotes/qtislam.html> (September 28, 2006).

4. Steve Inskeep, "Analysis: Start of Ramadan presents dilemma for U.S. commanders," transcript from National Public Radio Show *Morning Edition*, October 15, 2004.

5. Ibid.

6. Tara Bahrampour, "Muslim Youth Find a Bridge in a U.S. Tradition: Scouting," *The Washington Post*, November 21, 2005, p. B–6.

7. Ibid.

8. Personal interview with Bushra Malik, December 2005.

FURTHER READING

Barnes, Trevor. *Islam: Worship, Festivals, and Ceremonies From Around the World.* New York: Kingfisher, 2005.

Conover, Sarah, and Freda Crane. *Ayat jamilah = Beautiful Signs: A Treasury of Islamic Wisdom for Children and Parents.* Spokane, Wash.: Eastern Washington University Press, 2004.

Ganeri, Anita. *Muslim Festivals Throughout the Year.* Mankato, Minn.: Smart Apple Media, 2003.

Khan, Rukhsana. *Muslim Child: Understanding Islam Through Stories and Poems.* Morton Grove, Ill.: Albert Whitman & Co., 2002.

Maqsood, Ruqaiyyah Waris. *Islamic Mosques.* Chicago, Ill.: Raintree, 2006.

Thompson, Jan. *Islam.* North Vancouver, B.C.: Whitecap Books, 2005.

Winter, T. J., and John A. Williams. *Understanding Islam and the Muslims.* Louisville, K.Y.: Fons Vitae, 2002.

Wolf, Bernard. *Coming to America: A Muslim Family's Story.* New York: Lee & Low, 2003.

INTERNET ADDRESSES

Holiday Fun: Ramadan
<http://www.primarygames.com/holidays/ramadan/ramadan.htm>

Learn more about Ramadan and play some games.

Ramadan on the Net
<http://www.holidays.net/ramadan/>

Read more about Ramadan.

INDEX